LUMBERJACKS OF THE NORTH WOODS

were a rough and ready lot, toughened by long hours of hard work in the pine-forested Lake States. They played hard, too, and when the week's work was finished, the shanties rocked with music and singing and laughter. Lumberjacks called their Saturday night party a "hurrah," and a hurrah was something to see!

These rough men had a language all their own, as colorful as their songs and tall tales. Their imagination could run as wild as the wilderness they logged.

In this vivid, authentic account of life in a logging camp, the ringing of axes, the buzzing of saws, and the warning cry of *Timber-rrrrr!* can be heard. Readers also get a taste of the most dangerous, difficult, and exciting job in lumbering—the log drive—with the rumble of thousands of logs as "river pigs" guide them down foaming rivers in the spring.

This book is one of the *How They Lived* series, developed by Garrard to give meaning to the study of American history. Young people will find a deeper understanding and more lasting appreciation of history and geography as they see life in the past through the eyes of those who lived it.

Lumberjacks of the North Woods

Lumberjacks of the North Woods

BY LILLIE PATTERSON

ILLUSTRATED BY VICTOR MAYS

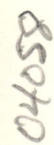

GARRARD PUBLISHING COMPANY
CHAMPAIGN, ILLINOIS

For Alex, Kevin, and Michael

Acknowledgements:

Duell, Sloan and Pearce, affiliate of Meredith Press, for "The Little Brown Bulls" from *Wisconsin Lore* by Robert E. Gard and L. B. Gorden. Copyright 1962 by Robert E. Gard and L. B. Gorden.

The University of Michigan Press for "Lumberjack's Alphabet," "The Shanty Boy in the Pines," "Lumberjack Chorus," "Bung Yer Eye," "Louie Sands and Jim McGee," "The Jam on Gerry's Rocks," and "Round River Drive" from *Songs of the Michigan Lumberjacks* by Earl Beck. Published in 1941 by University of Michigan Press.

Picture credits:

Culver Pictures: p. 73
Grand Rapids Museum: p. 31
Historical Pictures Service: p. 20, 42
Michigan Historical Commission: p. 1, back cover
Picture Collection, New York Public Library: p. 2, 5, 10, 29, 63, 65, 67
Red Keg Press, Bay City, Michigan: p. 34 (bottom)
State Historical Society of Wisconsin: p. 12, 15, 16, 17, 18, 25, 26, 27, 30, 32, 41, 47, 57, 60, 67, 74, 80, 83

Endsheets: Paintings by Victor M. Casenelli.
National Lumberman's Bank and
Trust Company, Muskegon, Michigan

Copyright © 1967 by Lillie Patterson
All rights reserved. Manufactured in the U. S. A.
Library of Congress Catalog Card Number: 67-14625

Contents

1. America Needed Lumberjacks 7
2. Laying Out the Lumber Camp 13
3. *Timber-rrrrr!* 20
4. Log Skidding 29
5. "Come and Get It!" 37
6. A Saturday Night Hurrah 45
7. Sunday and Sky Pilots 56
8. The Spring Log Drive 65
9. A Spree in Town 77
10. The Greatest Lumberjack of All . . 85
    Glossary 94
    Index 95

1. America Needed Lumberjacks

> Come, all ye gallant lumberers,
>   that range the wild woods through,
> Where the river flows and the timber grows
>   we're bound with a jolly crew;
> For the music of the mills is stopped
>   by the binding frost and snow;
> So we'll take our packs upon our backs,
>   and a-lumbering we'll go.
>
> *Old Lumberjack Song*

Far up in the North Woods, among the silvery lakes, there once walked a man called Paul Bunyan. Legend tells us that the many lakes there were made by his giant footprints. Legend also tells us that it was Paul Bunyan who invented logging.

7

Paul Bunyan did some of his most amazing logging during the Year of the Two Winters. The temperature stood two feet below zero that year. Water froze so fast that the ice was too hot to handle. Flames froze in the fireplace.

Words froze as fast as they were spoken. Lumberjacks did not write a single letter that winter. They just talked into sacks, tied the sacks tight, and sent them to their home folks. When the sacks were thawed out, the folks got all of the news. Songs froze too. When spring came, the North Woods rang with the beauty of thawed-out singing.

Paul Bunyan and his mighty lumberjacks logged the forests of Michigan, Minnesota, and Wisconsin. Pine trees were tall, lakes were large, men were strong, and snows were deep. "This is the country to grow up in," Paul Bunyan said. "This is the REAL AMERICA."

Those lumberjacks who created the Paul Bunyan tales also helped to create a mighty nation. America needed lumberjacks. Early American villages, towns, and cities were built chiefly of lumber. Lumberjacks cleared land for crops. They gave settlers the lumber they needed for homes, furniture, tools, and countless things they had to have for everyday living.

Many streams and rivers flowed through Lake States. These made it possible for lumberjacks to move logs cut during the winter to lumber towns like Saginaw and Peshtigo. Hundreds of sawmills there cut these logs into lumber.

A pioneer felled pines in this forest to clear land for his crops and to provide logs for a cabin.

The most useful tree was the white pine. It was light in weight, yet very strong. It split easily and smoothly, and it could be used by settlers who were not carpenters.

For many years, the forests of New England, New York, and Pennsylvania furnished all the white pine needed. Then in the middle of the nineteenth century, great numbers of people began to move West. Thousands of pioneers flocked to settle the treeless prairie region of the Midwest. These pioneers needed lumber, and they needed it in a hurry. Towns and cities were springing up overnight.

Lumbermen looked for a new supply of white pine. They found it in three of the Lake States. Some of the most magnificent forests in America stretched across Michigan, Wisconsin, and Minnesota. White pine grew in abundance.

These forests became known as the Pineries, or North Woods. The men who cut the pine soon became known as pinery-boys, shanty-boys, loggers, and later, as lumberjacks. The word "jack" means a man or a boy.

Lumberjacks came from all over the world to cut the pine in the Lake States. From 1850 to 1900 they gave young America the lumber it needed for building. Their exciting way of living and working was different from that of any other group of American pioneers.

The Cruiser by Marie Block

2. Laying Out the Lumber Camp

It took many types of lumberjacks to get the white pine from the forests to the people. The first lumberjacks to enter the forest wilderness were the timber cruisers. These men were expert woodsmen who explored unknown forests to find good tracts of pine trees. Some explored alone. Others took guides and helpers. Indians, who knew the forests well, often went along as guides.

When a cruiser found a good timber tract, he raced to find a government land office. He recorded the tract in the name of his employer, usually a lumber company.

Next, the lumber company made plans to build a camp and bring in lumberjacks. The timber cruiser helped to pick the best spot for the camp, near the center of the tract.

In late summer or early fall, other types of lumberjacks came to put up the city, as they called building the camp. This crew included a foreman, called bull of the woods; carpenters, called wood butchers; and blacksmiths, called iron burners. Lumberjacks made up a language of their own. They gave imaginative names to almost everything in their camp life.

The lumber camps, or logging camps, were needed only until the pine was cut. They were practical, not pretty. Camps differed from place to place, and from time to time. When logging crews were small, many camps had only one big building. After 1850, camps were built to house 50 or more lumberjacks.

In laying out a lumber camp, the foreman and the carpenter remembered old lumberjack superstitions. Floor boards should not be laid running toward the door. All trees leaning toward the camp should be cut. Nothing must be built from the wood of the poplar tree which was considered unlucky. Bad luck would follow a camp that overlooked such beliefs, it was said.

Horses draw a sledful of supplies into a Wisconsin lumber camp in this drawing by a camp cook in 1877.

The camp buildings were made of logs. The main building was the bunkhouse, also called the shanty. Camps with over a hundred men had two or more bunkhouses. Small windows at each end and a skylight let in air and light. The long side walls were needed for the bunks.

The box-like bunks were all double-deckers. There were two types. The lumberjacks named them after two types of guns. The bunks built from the walls toward the center of the floor were muzzle loaders. Sleepers crawled in head-first on their hands and knees. The bunks built along the walls like pullman car berths were

15

breech loaders. Sleepers crawled into them sideways. Carpenters used the wood of cedar trees for bunks whenever possible. Cedar kept away lice and bedbugs.

The carpenters built a long bench at the edge of the bunks. It ran around the bunkhouse. This was called the deacon seat. It took the place of chairs.

Other camp buildings were a cook shanty, a crude carpenter shop, a blacksmith shop, a barn, and a stable. A special building doubled as the camp office and supply store.

While some of the men put up the buildings, others made the roads. Tote roads were needed

Crosscut saws to cut the giant pines and cant hooks to roll logs onto sleds were sharpened by blacksmiths.

so that teams could tote, or bring in supplies. A main logging road was needed to take the logs from the forest to the river. A network of smaller trails led to the main logging road. The roads were made before the snow and ice of winter set in.

By the end of September, the camp buzzed with loud noises and bustled with workers. The carpenters and blacksmiths began building huge sleighs. Teamsters toted in supplies of all kinds: barrels of food, big stoves, shiny tools, heavy clothing. Other teamsters arrived, driving horses and oxen. Tools were sharpened. The chief cook came.

A traveling photographer took this picture of some lumberjacks and their tools in front of a bunkhouse. Even the camp animals were included in the picture.

By the first snowfall, the camp came to full life. The main crew of lumberjacks swaggered in. Some were seasoned lumberjacks who had followed the pine from the Eastern States to the Lake States. Many were farmers who worked as lumberjacks after they had harvested their crops. Others hoped to earn money to buy farms and work animals. Some of them were young men seeking adventure and fortune. Almost all of these men were Americans.

But thousands of immigrants worked as lumberjacks, too. Many came from Canada.

Others came from Europe, especially from the Scandinavian countries. The Irishmen, Germans, Frenchmen, Englishmen, Belgians, Poles, and Scotsmen—all helped to log the Lake States. The jabber of their different languages and accents added to the excitement.

Each lumberjack arrived in camp swinging a turkey sack. This was their name for the bags in which they kept their personal belongings. Each man gathered a pile of hay, straw, or evergreen boughs to spread over his bunk. He covered this with a blanket to make a mattress. There were no sheets. Stuffed sacks or coats served for pillows.

The lumberjacks rolled up in heavy blankets and hit the hay early. Snow was falling. It was time to start logging. The woods would be free from deer flies and mosquitoes. Snow and ice made the moving of logs easier. Snowtime meant logging time in the Lake States.

3. *Timber-rrrrr!*

A is for axes you very well know.
B is for the boys who use them just so.
C is for chopping, and now I'll begin. And
D is for danger we often are in.
E is for echoes that through the woods ring.
F is for foreman, the head of the thing.

Lumberjack's Alphabet

A blast from a long tin horn began a day in the bunkhouse. "Roooooll out! Daylight in the swamp. Roll out or roll up, boys!"

The awakening cry came from the camp handyman, called the bull cook. He blew the horn, called Gabriel, about four-thirty in the morning. The bull cook lit the kerosene lamps which hung on the bunkhouse walls. He put more wood in the big iron stove, known as the caboose.

The lumberjacks sat on the deacon seat and dressed for work. Their big problem was to keep warm and dry. They pulled on a heavy outside shirt over their woolen underwear. Some men wore gray shirts. Others wore gay plaids. Heavy pants were held up by suspenders. Most of the lumberjacks' outer clothing was made from Mackinaw cloth. This was heavy wool, often woven into bright plaids. Mackinaw material was used widely by lumberjacks and Indians in the Northwest.

Lumberjacks wore two or more pairs of wool knit socks. Their high boots were laced almost to their knees. Many lumberjacks wore a kind of moccasin with high uppers. These were made large enough so that many pairs of socks could be worn inside. Moccasins gave the feet more freedom, old lumberjacks said. They also helped to keep the feet from freezing in below-zero weather.

The outer coats were long double-breasted Mackinaw jackets. Hats, too, had to be warm. Some jacks liked hats made from the pelts of such animals as the fox or the muskrat. Others wore knitted stocking-caps that could be pulled down over the ears. Woolen mittens completed the outfit.

Everyone was dressed by five o'clock. Gabriel was blown again. The lumberjacks trudged through the pre-dawn darkness to the cook shanty. They ate their breakfast hurriedly and silently. Then they left the shanty. When daylight touched the forest, they were at work.

Lumbering needed the cooperation of many men. The lumberjacks were divided into crews. Each crew had a special job and needed special skills. The foreman directed all crews. Lumberjacks liked a foreman who could out-work any man in the woods. They wanted him to be kind, yet tough enough to lick any jack who gave trouble. The lumberjacks delighted in bragging about the deeds of their foremen, often in story and song.

The felling of a tree was an art. The pines towered over a hundred feet in the air, with trunks so thick that three men could scarcely reach around them. Skill was needed to keep falling trees from crushing other workers or harming nearby trees. "We can fell a tree in a high wind and drive a stake into the ground with it," lumberjacks boasted.

The men who chopped down the pine trees were called fallers. They worked in pairs. First, they chipped a V-shaped cut deep into the tree trunk. This showed the direction the tree must fall. They began sawing from the side opposite this notch.

The fallers worked silently and steadily, one at each end of a crosscut saw. Z-Z-Z! Z-Z-Z! The shiny saw teeth bit into the soft pine. The workers swayed in a see-saw rhythm with their feet planted firmly in the snow. Their warm breath turned to white fog in the cold air. Tiny icicles formed on their beards.

At just the right moment, the fallers placed a wedge into the saw cut. This protected the saw and started the tree falling in the right direction. *Crack!* A sound like a gunshot came from the tree.

"Timber-rrrrr! Down the line!" Loudly, the familiar warning cry of the lumberjacks echoed over the snow-frosted air. Nearby workers scampered to safety.

The towering pine tree trembled and leaned forward, gently, gracefully at first. Then with a tremendous crash, it toppled to the ground. Snow, sawdust, and pine needles whirled through the air. Lumberjacks always let out

Sturdy buckers cut this tall pine into logs with a crosscut saw so that it can be moved out of the forest.

a shout of excitement at this breathless sight.

A crew of swampers rushed to the fallen tree. They trimmed away the tops and branches. They needed skill to keep from harming the precious trunk. The swampers also swamped, or cleared the forest floor.

A crew of buckers sawed, or bucked the tree trunk into logs. Pine logs were about sixteen feet long. Standing trees are timber. When the trees are cut into lengths, they become logs. The logs are later sawed into lumber.

At noon a blast from Gabriel called the scattered lumberjacks to dinner. If lumberjacks worked a mile or less from camp, they walked

Tired lumberjacks eat their dinner in the woods. The hot food was brought to them in the box at the left.

to the cook shanty. Otherwise, the bull cook brought the dinner on a bobsled. The steaming food came in huge lard cans, or in big boxes covered with blankets.

One of the loggers had already trampled away snow, built a roaring fire, and heated water for tea. The lumberjacks pulled off their mittens and stretched their cold fingers over the blaze. They filled tin plates with steaming food and ate standing around the fire. They ate quickly to keep the food from freezing on their plates, or on their long beards.

The day wore on with the rhythmic ringing of axes, singing of saws, crunching of snow, and crashing of tall pines. Snow wove a white blanket against the deep green forest. By day's end, the lumberjacks were as snow-silvered as the trees and bushes.

Logging was a dawn-to-dusk job. When the men returned to the bunkhouse, the cook had a smoking-hot supper ready. The bull cook had the caboose glowing cherry-red. The weary men peeled off their wet clothes and hung them on drying wires strung around the bunkhouse. Each man had a special place to hang his clothes so that he could find them quickly in the morning.

Wet socks hang overhead to dry as jacks shed their boots and relax in bunks and on the deacon seat.

The lumberjacks put on bedroom shoes made out of cut-down old boots. They lit up their pipes and sat on the deacon seat to relax. This was the time for singing and for storytelling. Many lumberjack tales and ballads were created at such times.

This was a time for talking and dreaming about the future. Family men talked about their homes and children. Young men dreamed aloud of owning a farm, or perhaps of one day becoming a wealthy timber king. Immigrant lumberjacks talked of life in their homelands across the ocean.

This was also a time for bragging about the logging feats of the day. How deep was the snow? Who cut the biggest pine? Which crew outworked the other? What daring deed had the foreman, the camp boss, done that day?

At nine o'clock, the bull cook gave his last call of the day. "Lights out! Turn in, boys!"

The lumberjacks crawled into their bunks and hunted hay. The shanty filled with the odor of drying woolens and the sound of loud snores. Owls hooted. Timber wolves howled in the distance. The forest lay peaceful in the darkness of night.

4. Log Skidding

> The choppers and the sawyers,
>   They lay the timber low.
> The skidders and the swampers,
>   They haul it to and fro.
> Next come the sassy loaders
>   Before the break of day:
> "Come, load up your teams, my boys!
>   And to the river haste away."
>
>   *The Shanty Boy in the Pines*

"Scoot her to the drink, boys!"

In lumberjack language this meant, "Haul the logs to the river." The heavy, bulky logs had to be transported by water to sawmills. Luckily, the Lake States had plenty of lakes,

Skidders and oxen stop to rest before dragging the next load of logs to a nearby loading point.

rivers, and streams. The Indian names for these states were well chosen. Michigan means "Great Water"; Minnesota means "Sky-colored Water"; and Wisconsin means "Gathering of the Waters."

The first problem was to get the logs from the forest to the logging road. This was done by men with horses or oxen. Lumberjacks were strong, healthy men. Others could not stand the bitter, below-zero cold, the harsh living conditions, and the long hours of hard work. Lumberjacks trained their minds and powerful muscles to work together. They did many jobs that heavy machinery does today.

The logs were dragged, or skidded, out of the forest by men called skidders. Sometimes they dragged the logs with heavy chains. More often they used a go-devil. A go-devil was a V-shaped dragging sled with a crossbar for holding the log. Both chains and go-devils were most often pulled by oxen.

The faithful oxen were well suited to logging. Oxen moved easily in deep snow. Their thick hides protected them against bruises from bushes. They lived on less feed than horses, and seldom got sick.

All day long the skidders guided the oxen and go-devils along the snow-covered skidding

Hard-working skidders have loaded these go-devils with logs. Horses will drag them out of the forest.

trails. The men matched their strides to the slow, steady movement of the oxen. The logs had to be snaked out one by one. They were stacked at loading points, called skidways, along the logging road.

The most exciting part of log skidding then began. Teamsters drove by in large logging sleighs. A crew of loaders, called cant hook men, rolled the logs onto the sleighs. They used a tool called a cant hook to roll and turn the logs with ease. These men had to have good balance and a sure sense of timing. They were known as Knights of the Crooked Steel.

Cant hooks and chains are used to hoist a log into place. The sky-loader helps from high atop the load.

The loading of a logging sleigh was a breathtaking sight. An expert lumberjack called a sky-loader or a top-decker stood atop the sleigh load. He directed the movements. This was a dangerous job. A misstep or misjudgment could mean death from shifting logs. Each crew of loaders tried to pile the sleigh higher and higher. They liked to send out what they called a world's record load.

Teamsters guided the sleighs down the road. They knew well the ways of the animals they drove. Oxen and horses used in logging were all well trained. Teamsters carried long whips, but they guided with their voices. "Haw, there!" "Hyah!" "Huddup, there!" "Gee!"

Teamsters also knew the logging road. When the road ran level, they sat motionless, smoking peacefully. When the sleigh moved downhill, it was a different story. Teamsters crouched over the loads, alertly watching the logs, the animals, the road.

A crew of road monkeys kept the logging road in order. These men used a huge water tank on a sled to sprinkle the road. The water froze to form a highway of solid ice, several inches thick. Animals needed only to tug gently on the big sleigh to haul tons of logs.

Horses moved better on icy roads; oxen moved better in snow.

On steep places, road monkeys spread hay, sand, or boughs to slow the sleigh. When a sleigh did run out of control, the falling logs killed or injured both animals and teamster.

Near the riverbank, every log had to be measured and branded. Lumber companies used brands called log marks. The log mark design was cut into the end of a heavy branding hammer. Strong lumberjacks swung the hammer and drove the marks deep into the ends of the pine logs. Lumbermen used log marks in the same way that cowboys used cattle brands. They were marks of ownership.

The branded logs were stacked in tiers along the riverbank. They stayed there for the winter, bound together by ice and propped up by timber.

Lumberjacks took pride in their work. Each crew tried to outwork the other. Wise foremen kept up a friendly spirit of competition. They encouraged contests of all kinds.

Log hauling was called log skidding. Log skidding contests were always exciting events. One lumberjack would brag: "I can skid a bigger load than any jack in camp!" Another jack would take up the dare. Then the foreman would arrange a contest to find the best man.

Each contestant chose several lumberjacks to help him. The other lumberjacks whooped and cheered as the men skidded as fast as they could. When the foreman called time, the logs were counted. The lumberjack who skidded the most logs won a prize, usually some tobacco.

"Hurrah!" his camp mates cried. "You're the best." It was not the prize, but the glory that a lumberjack wanted. "You're the best!"

The fun often ended with the singing of ballads written about these skidding contests. Lumberjacks changed the names of people and places in their ballads to fit people and places they knew.

A favorite ballad was "The Little Brown Bulls." It describes a contest between McClusky's team of white spotted steers, and Gordon's team of little brown bulls. The contest goes on:

> McClusky, the Scotsman,
>   showed nothing like fear,
> As he cried, "Whoa hush!"
>   to the white spotted steers!
> For it's on, boys, and gone, boys!
>   Take hold of the snow!
> We're hooked to the log,
>   and now let 'em go!
>
> Bull Gordon he worked
>   with a pipe in his mouth,
> And the wind blew the smoke
>   from the North to the South.
> Says he to his helper,
>   "John, I'm scared as can be
> That those white spotted steers
>   are too much for me!"

The ballad ends with Gordon the winner and the shanty ringing with his praises. After each stanza of such ballads, lumberjacks shouted out a chorus:

> Derry-down-down-down, derry down.

5. "Come and Get It!"

"Heigh-derry! Ho-derry! Hey-derry-down!
Give a shanty boy grub and nothing goes wrong."

Lumberjack Chorus

"The secret of success in the woods is well-fed men," wrote a wise old lumberman. A well-fed crew was a happy, hard-working crew.

A good cook was as important to a lumber camp as a good foreman. The foreman was camp boss, but the cook ruled as kingbee in the kitchen. Lumberjacks readily came to work for camps that had good cooks. Hard work in the pine-scented air gave the jacks enormous appetites.

They were never slow in "walking" the cook if his food failed to please them. "He's a stomach robber," they'd say. One morning when the foreman opened the bunkhouse door, the lumberjacks would kick it shut again. "We need a new cook!" they would cry.

The foreman knew that the lumberjacks would not work if the cook stayed. He would go to the cook and tell him, "Pack your turkey and hit the hay trail. Here's your time."

Sometimes it was the cook who became displeased. He would go to the foreman. "Make her out, boss. I'm going to mix me up a walk." He meant, "I'm quitting!"

The cook shanty was divided into a kitchen and a room for eating. A great iron stove took up half of the kitchen. On top were griddles for making pancakes, called flapjacks. The cook had helpers, called cookees, to make flapjacks by the hundreds.

A. S. Draper, a famous lumberman, once worked as a cook's helper. He later described how stacks of flapjacks were made. Three cookees worked as a team. One kept the fire roaring in the wood-burning stove. One poured the batter. The other flipped the flapjacks and tossed them into a big dishpan. Molasses for flapjacks was bought in barrels. Large camps used two or more barrels a month.

When cooks made bread, they mixed a big batch of dough. They saved part of the dough for the next day. This is why lumberjacks called bread sourdough. They called camp cooks Sourdough Stiffs or Baking Powder Bums.

Lumberjacks loved sweets. They needed lots of sweets to give them energy. Pies were popular. Some were made from dried fruits. Others were made from vinegar, sugar, water, and cornstarch. These tasted much like modern butterscotch pies.

One logger remembered that each pie was cut into huge slices when served. Cooks also baked gingerbread, cakes, doughnuts, and big cookies. The cookies were so big and round that lumberjacks called them stovelids.

Salt pork, beans, potatoes, dried fruits, and homemade bread provided the main food. Such provisions could be bought in large amounts and stored for long periods. Lumber camps had trouble getting fresh meats and vegetables. There were few farmers nearby. Food supplies had to be brought in over difficult routes. Lumberjacks sometimes fished and hunted so that they could have fresh meat.

Food orders were large. An order for a Minnesota camp included 200 barrels of flour, 104 barrels of salt pork, 9000 pounds of sugar, 1100 pounds of tea, 1700 pounds of dried apples, and 1900 pounds of tobacco.

The lumberjacks entertained themselves by making up humorous names for their foods. Flapjacks were hotboys. Tea was belly wash. Coffee was swamp water. Biscuits were sinkers. Prunes were called logging berries because they were served so often.

Lumberjacks also poked fun at their food in stories and rhymes:

> Tread on my corns and tell me lies,
> But don't feed me dried apple pies.

Mealtime in a lumber camp was a sight that visitors never forgot. The cookees blew a few blasts on Gabriel. The cook opened the shanty door and bellowed the famous call to meals: "Come and get it!" The jacks dropped whatever they were doing and rushed to the cook shanty. They knew that the cook meant business when he shouted, "Eat up or I'll throw it out."

Cooks, cookees, and fiddlers pose before well-loaded tables in the cook shanty of a large Wisconsin camp. Posters advertising plays decorate the wall.

The lusty lumberjacks filed in meekly and took seats on benches built along the two sides of long tables. Each man took the same seat for every meal. Each newcomer stood quietly beside the door until the cook gave him a seat.

The cookees had the oilcloth-covered tables already set. Plates, cups, knives, forks, and spoons were all made from tin. "Shoot on the eats!" the cookees called out. Tinware clattered as lumberjacks piled their plates with food. After that, the only sounds were the chomping of jaws, the scraping of tinware, and the

42

scurrying feet of cookees as they refilled empty dishes.

The cook had set strict rules for mealtimes. Everyone, even the camp owner, obeyed these rules: No hats on at the table! Every man in his own seat! No talking while eating!

All camps kept the "no talking while eating" rule. It saved time. It kept down the babel of many different languages being spoken at once. Above all, it kept the boisterous jacks in check. They could become as playful as children. If they talked, they joked. If they joked, they romped. The air might soon be filled with food and flying tinware.

The lumberjacks finished eating in fifteen minutes. The cookees cleaned up and started getting ready for the next meal. Indians sometimes crept silently up to the cook shanty to look for leftover food put outside by cookees. Indian hunting grounds had become logging tracts; their fishing streams were now log highways. They had a hard time finding food. Indians were usually too proud to beg, but they accepted food left for them. Lumberjacks knew that friendship was the unspoken thanks given in return for the food.

Wild animals also visited the lumber camps.

Bears were as fond of sweets as lumberjacks. Every spring they came to lick the empty barrels that still held drops of molasses. Deer and porcupines liked a salty flavor. They licked the barrels in which salt pork had been bought. Chipmunks came to gnaw on the piles of prunestones.

The growth of railroads after 1870 brought many changes in logging. It also brought better food for the lumberjacks. Canned goods were used. Fresh meats and vegetables were brought in. The cook still called, "Come and get it!" But the lumberjacks got a wider and tastier choice of what they called grub.

6. A Saturday Night Hurrah

It was Saturday night in LS Camp No. 8. Lumber camps were known by numbers and by the names of their owners. LS stood for Louie Sands. This camp owner had come from Sweden. He had worked as a lumberjack, saved his money, and bought tracts of pine. In the 1880's, he owned several camps.

The week's work at Camp 8 was over. It was time for fun. Nels Fredrickson, the best fiddler in camp, tuned up his fiddle-box. Ole

Johnson pecked away on the strings of his dulcimer. Pete Carlson, the cook, blew on his beloved mouth organ.

The musicians swung from one rollicking tune to another. Some of the jacks jumped up and started dancing. The dancing led to singing. Soon the shanty rocked with merriment.

The fiddler struck up the German folk tune, "O Tannenbaum." Every jack to a man burst into his favorite song about beans.

> Who feeds us beans? Who feeds us tea?
>   Louie Sands and Jim McGee.
> Who thinks that meat's a luxury?
>   Louie Sands and Jim McGee.
> We make the big trees fall ker-splash
> And hit the ground an awful smash;
> And for the logs who gets the cash?
>   Louie Sands and Jim McGee.

The song suddenly stopped. The bunkhouse filled with the silence of surprise. In the door stood Louie Sands. The camp owner was tall and handsome, with curly hair, reddish-brown beard, and a walrus mustache.

"Would Louie be angry because they poked fun at him in their song?" the lumberjacks wondered. No! Louie smiled and pointed to

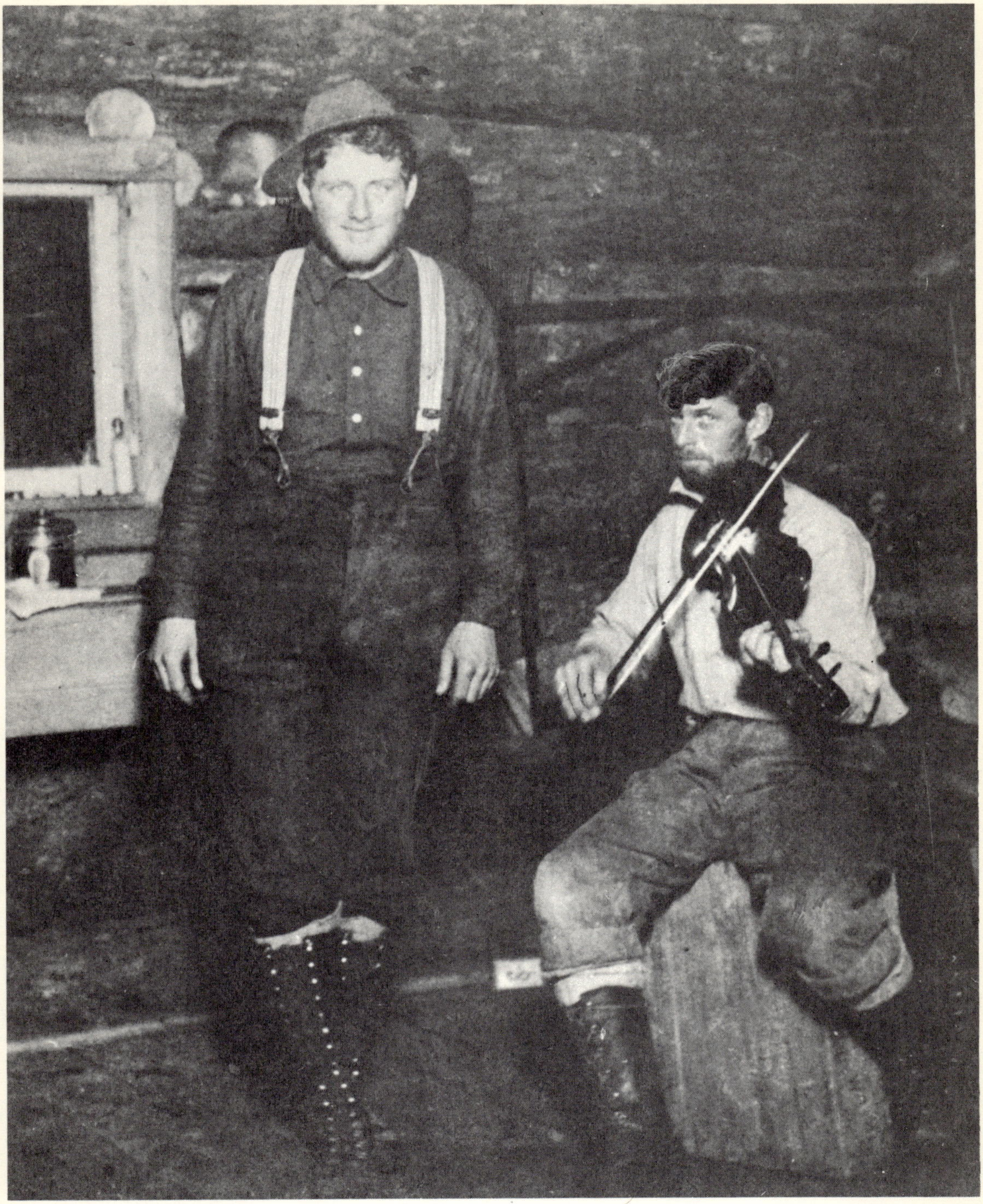

the musicians. His powerful voice led the jacks in booming out the remaining verses:

> Who feeds us beans until we're blue?
>   Louie Sands and Jim McGee.
> Who thinks that nothing else will do?
>   Louie Sands and Jim McGee.
> Who gives us beans three times a day
> And gives us very little pay?
> Who gives us beans, again I say?
>   Louie Sands and Jim McGee.

Rolland Maybee described this party in his book, *Michigan's White Pine Era, 1840–1900*. Many other old lumberjacks wrote or told of such parties. Lumberjacks called a Saturday night party a hurrah. As did other American pioneers, they made entertainment out of what was at hand.

A Saturday night hurrah was something to see! A lively lumberjack volunteered to be caller for the evening: "Make way for a stag dance!" he shouted. Half of the jacks quickly tied a handkerchief around one arm. This made them the ladies, or gals. The other jacks were the gents, or bucks.

The hurrah grew hilarious. Faster and faster screeched the fiddle. Around and around whirled the bucks and their gals. Swinging, shuffling, and stomping, they kept up with the music.

Unshaven, 200-pound lumberjacks swung one another until the shanty walls shivered.

The caller waved to the fiddler. "Let's have some solo dancing!" Now immigrant lumberjacks showed off the dances from their native countries. There were country dances, cotillions, polkas, reels, jigs, and quadrilles.

"Where's the greenhorn?" the caller cried out. Greenhorns were new lumberjacks. They had to take the first turn at being "It" in Saturday night games.

"Shuffle the Brogue" was a favorite lumberjack game. The word "brogue" is an Irish name for a shoe. A circle of players sat on the floor, knees drawn up, hands behind them. The greenhorn sat in the center. The players passed an old shoe behind their backs. "Shove! Shove! Shove!" they shouted.

When the greenhorn turned around to look for the shoe, the player holding it gave him a whack. The greenhorn had to catch a jack holding the shoe before he could trade places with him.

"Kick the Bucket" was another popular game. "Stand with your back to the wall," the jacks would tell a greenhorn. "Let's see how far you can jump." They marked the spot where he landed. "Now, see if you can jump backward to the wall." Meanwhile, someone slipped a bucket behind the greenhorn. Then when he started to jump backward, he scooted on the bucket out into the room.

The other jacks doubled over with laughter. It is said that the expression, "kicked the bucket," came from this game.

Everyone was expected to join in the hurrah. Those who took no part had to pay a fine. "Sweeten the poor box!" the others demanded. Any lumberjack who broke a camp rule had to put a pound of tobacco in the bunkhouse poor box. Tobacco in this box was free to all.

A hurrah was a time for louse races. Most

bunkhouses were bothered by lice. Lumberjacks folded a piece of paper into equal lengths. This was the racetrack. Two jacks faced each other. Each started his louse from the outer end toward the center fold. The other men formed a circle around them, taking sides and making bets. The first louse to reach the center of the paper was cheered as the winner.

A hurrah was a time for making up songs too. Music was almost as important in a lumber camp as food. Any jack who could fiddle or sing well was a big hit. Foremen made sure to hire at least one good singer for each camp. Lumberjacks classified singers into two types: wailers and bullroarers. Camps needed both.

"Let's have a song match!" someone would yell. The lumberjacks divided themselves into two singing groups. Each group chose a leader. Each side had solos as well as group singing.

The other side sometimes shouted encouragement: "Good boy!" "A bully song, and well sung!" "Good haul for the push!"

The playful jacks could quickly change the prideful cheers to teasing: "Cheese the racket, chummy!" "You've got a good voice for pork and beans!"

Lumberjacks called out for their favorite

ballads: "Give us 'Bung Yer Eye'!" It took a bullroarer to lead the rousing ballads.

> I love a girl in Saginaw;
>   She lives with her mother.
> I defy all Michigan
>   To find such another.
> She's tall and slim, her hair is red,
>   Her face is plump and pretty.
> She's my daisy Sunday best-day girl,
>   And her front name stands for Kitty.
>
>   *Chorus*
> Bung yer eye! Bung yer eye!

The wailers led the sad ballads. The husky lumberjacks wiped tears from their eyes as they sang of love, death, injuries, hardships, and loneliness. They spoke the closing lines of ballads to show that the song was ended.

A hurrah was a time for making up stories as well as songs. A special spot on the deacon seat became the throne on which the storyteller sat. He could stay there only so long as he held the interest of his listeners.

Lumberjack storytellers had vivid imagination, remarkable memory, and a keen sense of humor. Their tales were chiefly tales of exaggeration.

Many tales were told to tease greenhorns. These tales were about fearsome beasts that prowled the North Woods, waiting to pounce upon lumberjacks. These tales also poked fun at the dangers and mysteries of forest living.

The hodag was the most famous of the fearsome creatures. "The hodag looks like a dinosaur, with a tail like a spear," lumberjacks told greenhorns. "You'll think a whole woods full of wildcats and hyenas are after you when you hear one."

When a lumberjack was killed or injured, the others would say, "The varmints got him!" What happened to the poor lumberjack who mysteriously disappeared? A whirling whumpus got him. This fearsome creature whirled in the tote road and smashed passing lumberjacks to jelly. Why was another jack injured by a falling tree branch? An agropelter, who lived in tree trunks, chunked the branch down upon him. And how did a greenhorn become frostbitten? He was bitten by frost-fleas or snow-snakes. The pink eyes of the deadly snow-snake could freeze a jack in his tracks.

Lumberjacks invented other creatures, all fearsome, and all funny. The axehandle hound sneaked into camps and ate the handles off lumbering tools. The hidebehind hid behind pine trees and pounced upon lumberjacks when they passed by. The tote-road shagamaws stole the many Mackinaw coats and mittens which lumberjacks found missing.

A Saturday night hurrah lasted until past midnight. Lumberjacks could sleep later on Sunday. This was the one day in the week when they saw daylight in the camp.

7. Sunday and Sky Pilots

"Boil 'em up alive, boys!"

Lumberjacks laughed and joked while they did their weekly laundry in the camp yard. They called Sunday boil-up day. Clothes had to be boiled to rid them of lice.

Barrels sawed in half served as washtubs. The jacks first scrubbed their clothes with strong yellow soap. They next built fires under huge tin lard cans. The clothes were dumped into the cans and boiled in soapy water mixed with lye.

The men hung their laundry on lines strung up in the yard. The clothes dried slowly, or sometimes froze quickly. In frigid weather, the laundry was hung on the drying wires in the bunkhouse.

Sunday was the only day that lumberjacks had to do their washing and cleaning. They cleaned out their bunks and tried to rid them of lice, which they called crumbs. They shook out the blankets and beat them with sticks called "crumb crushers." Sometimes they threw out the old hay and straw and put in a fresh supply.

Lumberjacks spruced themselves up. They combed their beards and cut each other's hair.

Burly lumberjacks help each other wring out clothes on washday in a lumber camp.

But most lumberjacks did not bother to shave during the logging season.

Sunday was the time to visit the "wanigan." This was the shanty used for the camp office and supply store. The name "wanigan" comes from a Chippewa Indian word meaning supplies.

The camp clerk was called an inkslinger. He ruled over the wanigan as the cook ruled over the kitchen. He kept a record sheet for each lumberjack. It showed the number of days the jack had worked and the purchases he had made from the wanigan. Lumberjacks bought everything on credit. They were paid about a dollar a day, but did not get their pay until the end of the logging season. The food and lodging were furnished free by the camp owner.

The wanigan sold supplies that lumberjacks needed while in camp. They bought Mackinaw clothing, mittens, socks, boots, needles, threads, and rubbing medicines. Nearly all lumberjacks bought smoking or chewing tobacco.

Sunday afternoon was the quietest time of the week. The lumberjacks dressed in clean clothes and relaxed on their bunks or on the deacon seat. Some smoked in silence. Some mended holes in their boots and clothing. Many wrote letters to their prized logs, as they called

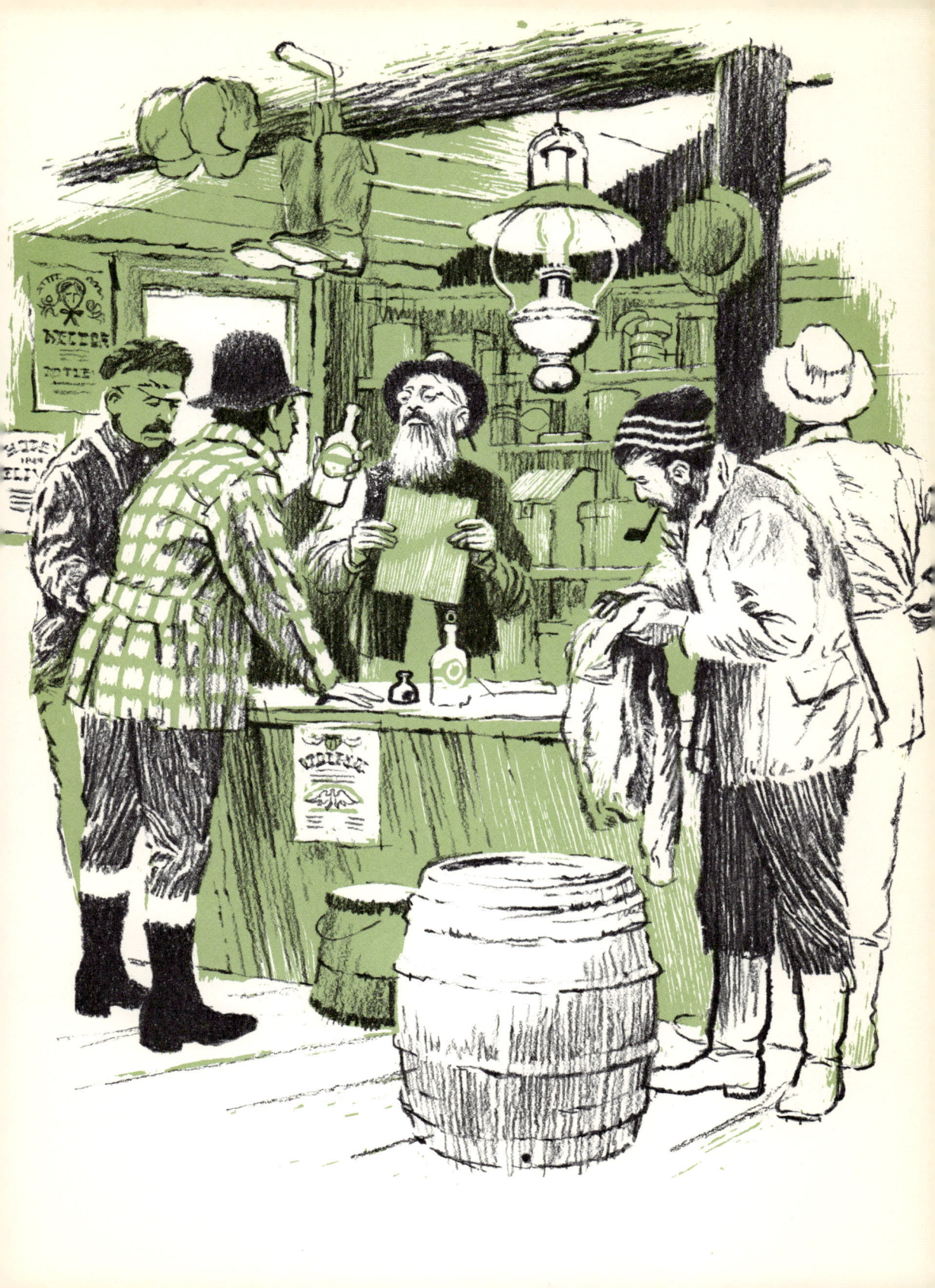

Sunday was a good day for a lumberjack to shave his beard, sharpen some tools, or read a well-worn book.

their wives and sweethearts. When lumberjacks finished their own letters, they wrote for buddies who had no schooling.

Later, the lumberjacks leafed through old magazines and newspapers. The *Police Gazette* was the favorite magazine in lumber camps. It had lots of pictures for those who could not read. Many of the immigrant loggers had not yet learned to read and speak English, even though they were schooled in their native language.

Sunday was the time to take care of health needs. The two most common complaints were scaly toes and chafed skin. These were brought on by spending long hours in wet clothes. Lumberjacks painted scaly toes with white lead, which was a popular remedy of that day. They sprinkled chafed skin with the dust of rotting pine. This worked like talcum powder.

Luckily, most of the men stayed healthy. The hardy life in the clear, crisp air gave them a physical fitness few men could boast. The camp foreman knew how to give first aid, and what to do for wounds made by sharp tools. Doctors were many miles from camp. Pioneer doctors braved many hardships to reach injured lumberjacks. They would travel by snowshoes, canoe, dog-team, horseback, and often on foot.

Dr. Frank Bohn of Seney, Michigan was one of these brave doctors. One day, Dr. Bohn was called to a camp forty-five miles from his home. A young lumberjack's leg had been crushed by a rolling log. Dr. Bohn packed his black bag, saddled his horse, and rode thirty miles. He traveled twelve miles by boat. A man with a team of horses met him and took him the rest of the way. The doctor treated the injured man and cured his leg. The young lumberjack lived to be a great-grandfather of many children.

Dr. Bohn went to another camp when a sky-loader was pinned beneath falling logs. Dr.

Bohn made a stretcher out of poles and camp blankets. Twelve lumberjacks walked along to carry the stretcher to a railroad boxcar. They held the stretcher during the rough ride in order to ease the loader's pain.

The nearest town had no hospital, so they took the injured man to a hotel room. Dr. Bohn put the broken body in a plaster of Paris cast. In spite of his pain, the young lumberjack smiled and joked. "Well, boys, this is the first time I was ever in Paris."

He lived. So did many others who seemed to be hurt beyond help. Doctors could not explain the miracles. The answer lay not only in the lumberjacks' physical fitness. It lay also in their belief in themselves. They lived close to nature, and took on some of nature's strength. Something which would seem impossible to an average man was simply a challenge to a lumberjack.

Sunday afternoon was a time when traveling preachers came. Lumberjacks called them sky pilots. These preachers visited lumber camps to hold religious services.

One of the best known sky pilots was Rev. Frank Higgins of Minnesota. He became a folk hero. Many legends tell of his deeds.

Rev. Higgins had the size and strength of a lumberjack. He often stayed in a lumber camp for several days and shared the work of the jacks. He later wrote, "I went out as a lumberjack, and did the things the men did." He trained many lumberjacks to work as sky pilots. He knew that lumberjacks readily took advice from men who talked their language and matched their skill.

Sky pilots did more than preach. They knew that many of the lumberjacks lived through the whole logging season without receiving a letter from anyone. Sky pilots encouraged the men to write to families and friends. They wrote letters for unschooled men. They gave news summaries of what was happening in the outside world, and left magazines and newspapers in the camps.

Like Sunday, Christmas Day was a time when logging stopped. Lumberjacks who lived close enough to their homes went to spend the holiday with their families. Others stayed in the shanty, or visited nearby camps. Christmas dinner was always a grand feast. "The cooks let themselves loose!" old lumberjacks recalled.

Christmas greetings were exchanged in a typical lumberjack style. "Merry Christmas, chummy!" one jack would call out.

"Thanks, pal!" another might answer. "I hope you live forever, and that I live to see you die."

After Christmas, lumberjacks logged harder than ever. The piles of logs at the riverbank rose thirty or more feet in the air. It was a race against time. Spring was coming. Spring brought an end to the cutting and hauling. It brought the beginning of the most exciting event in lumbering—the log drive.

8. The Spring Log Drive

Spring came to the woods. Soft rain and sun melted the snow. The foreman watched the river rise higher and higher. "She's coming, boys!" he cried.

The sawing and skidding stopped. The jacks got ready for the spring log drive. There were no railroads or big trucks to take the winter's cut to sawmills. The logs had to be floated down-river. The big logs floated as easily as cork.

Lumberjacks who guided, or drove the logs called themselves river pigs. Only the top lumberjacks became river pigs. Log driving was the most dangerous and difficult job in lumbering.

Everyone in camp prepared to move in the spring. Men who did not go with the drive went on to do other work. Many worked on farms, in mines, or in sawmills. Some traveled to towns for a spring spree.

The cook packed to move. The drive kitchen was a shack on a floating raft. It was called a wanigan because it also carried supplies. On big drives several wanigans were needed, since there were often a hundred or more river pigs.

The river swelled to a churning pitch, called a "driving pitch." It made logs float easily and fast. The foreman gave the signal: "Drive her, boys! She's wheeling!"

The river pigs were raring to go. "Hi! Now for some *real* work." They put on cotton overalls that were light when wet, and quick to dry. Their high boots had spikes, or calks fastened to the heels and soles. They wore old hats cocked to one side.

The piles of branded logs which were stacked in tiers along the riverbank had to be freed. Top river pigs carefully chopped away the props and remaining ice. The whole winter's cut rolled into the water. The earth shook with the thunder of thousands of logs falling. Splashing sprays shot skyward. The strong current sent the logs spinning downstream. The drive was on.

The river pigs jumped atop the floating pine. Their needle-sharp calked boots kept them from slipping off the wet logs. The main driving tools were the peavey and the pike pole. Both had long steel points for guiding the logs. The peavey was named for Joseph Peavey, the Maine blacksmith who invented it.

As the sea of logs spread out over several miles, the men worked in crews. The crew in front guided the drive in the right direction, and kept the logs moving with the current. Another crew worked in the middle of the drive to keep the logs from jamming up. The rear crew used the long pike poles to push straying logs back into the current.

Farmers and townfolks came from miles around to watch the drama of the drive. Children looked on as excitedly as though they were viewing a circus parade. Boys dreamed of growing up to become famous river pigs.

Sometimes the scene was peaceful. The logs floated as gracefully and swiftly as arrows. River pigs stuck their peaveys into the giant logs and rode them as easily as though they were gentle ponies. Other river pigs walked and watched along the shore, like policemen patrolling a peaceful beat.

The scene became noisy and busy when the logs turned and twisted and tumbled about. River pigs used their spikes as spears. They dashed from log to log, corralling them as though they were cowboys driving a herd of cattle. Their bodies heaved and swayed with the bucking logs as they rode them. The rear

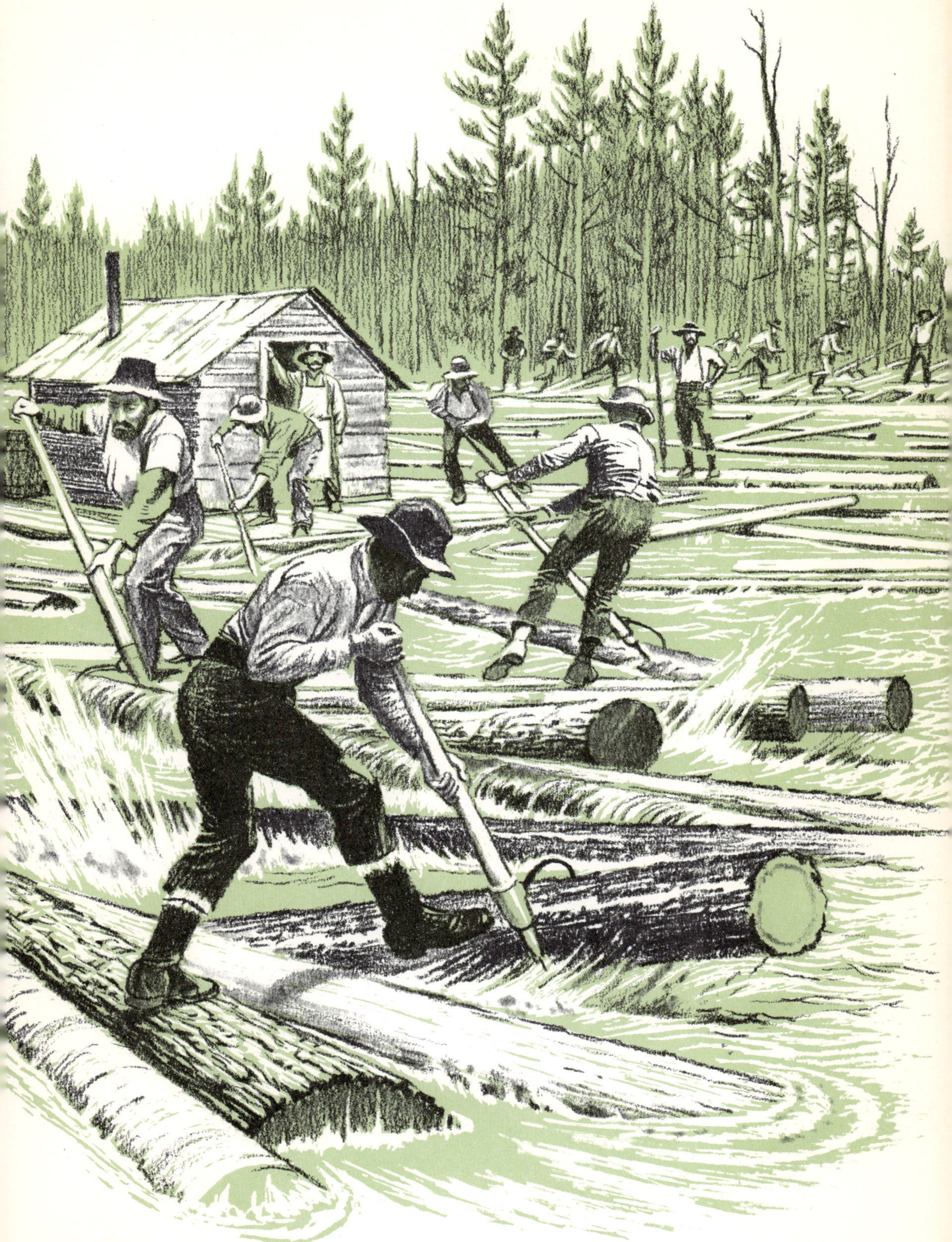

crew worked waist-deep in water rounding up runaway logs that were stranded in the bushes or on the riverbank.

Boom! Boom! Boom! sounded the logs as they ground together. *Clank! Clank! Clank!* answered the peaveys as the river pigs pried logs apart. Above these sounds could be heard commands, questions, directions, and warnings, shouted in a half-dozen different languages.

The river pigs were good and they knew it. "Catty on the calks!" they bragged. "You can throw a bar of yellow soap into the river, and a river pig will ride the bubbles to shore."

These log drivers lived in constant danger of death from drowning or being crushed by logs. Their clothes stayed sopping wet. Yet, they joked while they worked. "You floated out from under your hat," they teased a buddy who fell into the water. They took no time to worry about the dangers and hardships. They took joy in the thrill and excitement of a job few men could do.

A fleet of bateaux floated along with each crew. The word *bateau* is French and means boat. Indians often handled these swift, slim, graceful boats on the drives. They could steer bateaux forward, backward, sideways, in all kinds of water. These bateaux carried men, tools, and supplies from one section to another as emergencies arose.

The hard-driving river pigs needed even more food than the woodsmen. The wanigan floated along with the main part of the drive whenever possible. The men ate four or five meals a day. Those who were near enough came to the wanigan to eat. The cook sent cookees slipping and sliding over logs to take food to others.

River pigs carried emergency food in lunch bags made of oilcloth or canvas. These were strapped to their backs. They called them nose bags. An old Wisconsin river pig remembered a drive when his crew did not see the wanigan

A wanigan follows the drive through dangerous rapids.

for three days. They could not stop to visit it because the logs were piling up.

When it became too dark to tell log from land, the men went to their wanigan for supper. After supper they smoked, and some of the river pigs hung up their clothes to dry. Others believed an old superstition: "If a river pig lets his clothes dry on his body, he will not get sick during the drive." They stretched out on the raft, in tents, or on the ground, and slept soundly. There was another superstition: "In the full of the moon the logs will float freely."

On nights when the logs threatened to pile up and stop moving, the foreman called the river pigs back to work. Log jams did form, however. It could happen at any time. The dreaded call came across the water. "Jam below!" Each crew echoed it to the men behind: "Jam below!"

The river pigs jumped to action. Now they really showed their agility, daring, and split-second timing. The men nearest to the jam worked frantically to untangle the logs. They whirled and whacked with their peaveys. They jumped from log to log and pried them apart. Every second counted. The logs behind could

The brave river pig who cuts the key log causing this log jam may be killed by the freed logs.

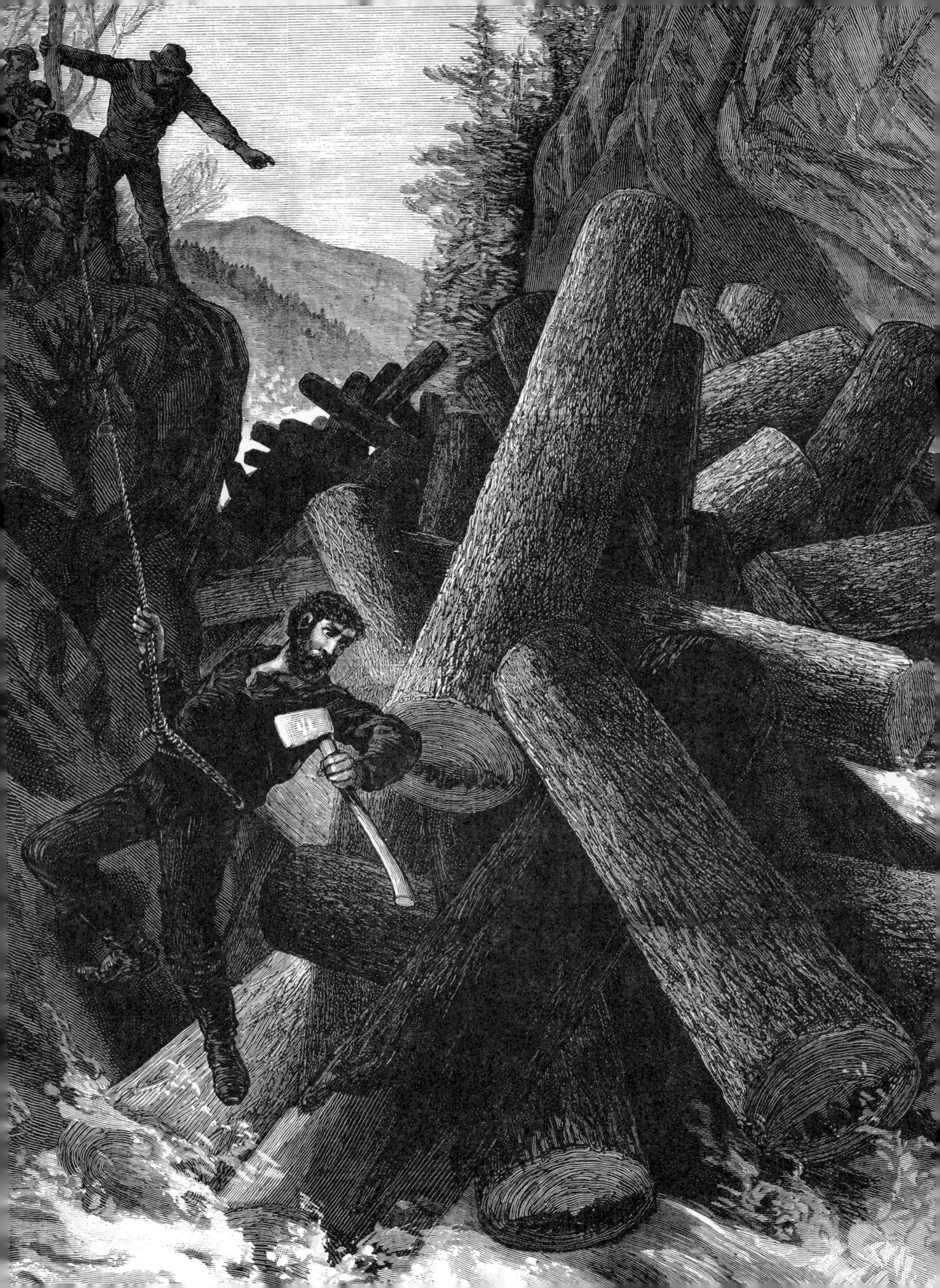

pound into those that had stopped and cause a bigger jam.

The great moment of danger came when a jam broke. The freed logs swept everything along with them. If a river pig did not jump away quickly enough, his body was ground beneath the flood of logs. His peavey floated away untouched. A dead man's peavey was jinxed, lumberjacks believed. They never used it again on that drive. Newspapers reported as many as five deaths a week for one drive.

Some jams formed too quickly to be broken by hand tools. Logs then stacked for miles upriver in a tangled jigsaw puzzle. River pigs worked night and day, taking little time for eating or sleeping.

Such jams had to be blasted free. The foreman sent to the wanigan for sticks of dynamite. He never had to order a river pig to place the dynamite. There were always volunteers.

The volunteer silently took the sticks of dynamite. He whispered a word of confidence to his buddies, and told them what to do with the things in his turkey if he did not return. He went out to what could be sudden death. But he was as calm as though he simply went to fell a tree.

Watchers along the shore held their breath. When the volunteer lit the fuse, everyone ducked. *Boom*! The dynamite exploded with a shattering roar and blasted a hole in the jam. The logs surged free.

Echoing cries came from the people watching from the shore when they saw the volunteer leap to safety. Men, women, and children waved hats, handerchiefs, and bonnets. Day after day they had come to watch the tense drama.

The foreman or volunteer who broke a big jam became a hero. Other lumberjacks told of his bravery in stories and ballads. "The Jam on Gerry's Rocks" is a ballad based on truth. Like many lumberjack songs, it begins with the words, "Come all ye . . ."

> Come all ye true-born shanty boys
>   whoever that ye be,
> I would have you pay attention
>   and listen unto me
> Concerning a young shanty boy,
>   so tall, genteel, and brave—
> 'Twas on a jam at Gerry's Rocks
>   he met his watery grave.

The sad ballad tells how six log-driving lumberjacks volunteered to help their young foreman break a log jam. They were all killed when the jam broke suddenly.

> They had not rolled off many logs
>   till Monroe to them did say,
> "I'd have you boys be on your guard:
>   that jam will soon give way."
> Scarce the warning had been spoken
>   when the jam did break and go,
> And it carried off those six brave youths
>   and their foreman, young Monroe.

Spring log drives lasted from 30 to 90 days. Drives ended when the logs reached a sorting boom. A boom was a floating corral made from logs or stout timber chained end-to-end. It penned the logs until they could be sorted by ownership log marks and taken to sawmills. A big drive often carried logs and lumberjacks from several camps.

As soon as a drive was over, the river pigs got their pay, and then it was time to treat themselves to a spree in town.

9. A Spree in Town

Lumber towns were called sawdust towns. They sprang up throughout the North Woods. Their sawmills cut the lumber that America needed. Their amusement places furnished entertainment for the lonely lumberjacks. Many of these towns developed into great cities.

Saginaw, Michigan was such a town. Along the great Saginaw River grew some of the best pine trees in the country. Saginaw looked like many other lumber towns. Sawdust seemed to be scattered everywhere. Rough pine-board sidewalks lined the muddy streets. Piles of drying lumber stretched along the docks. A person could walk twelve miles or more on stacks of lumber without touching the ground. There were the usual hotels, rooming houses, grocery stores, bank, post office, and many, many saloons.

After the spring drive Saginaw leaped into life. More than a hundred sawmills whined and buzzed day and night. Their towering smokestacks dotted the banks of the river. Steamers, tugboats, barges, rafts, schooners, bateaux, all brought in supplies. They took out lumber and lumber products for all parts of the world.

When the lumberjacks hit town they cashed their checks. Some rushed to mail money to their families. Each man kept back some money to treat the boys. There were always some lumberjacks who kept up a spending spree until their hard-earned money was gone.

The men headed for hotels and rooming houses. They got shaves, haircuts, and baths. They bought new clothes, but kept on their boots as a sign of their toughness. These calked boots clattered on the board sidewalks as the jacks swaggered along, kicking splinters from the white pine planks. French Canadians wore dashing red sashes around their waists. Townfolks nicknamed lumberjacks "The Red Sash Brigade."

Lumberjacks played as hard as they logged. For months they had worked at big, noisy jobs. Now they wanted noisy, boisterous entertainment.

Fighting to show how tough they were was a form of entertainment jacks enjoyed. They had their own fighting codes, though. They seldom used knives or guns. Their weapons were their fists, teeth, heads (for butting), and feet (calked boots and all). After a fight there was no anger. The winner was best man. That was that.

Every camp had its champion fighter. The most famous of all lumberjack fighters was

Paul Bunyan and Hels Helsen are said to have fought for days to decide who was the better man.

Silver Jack. "The fightin'est man in the Saginaw Valley," jacks called him. Silver Jack is the subject of many ballads and legends.

People in lumber towns held many kinds of contests to entertain lumberjacks. Everyone knew that these men liked games that tested strength, endurance, and skill. There were chopping, sawing, climbing, pulling, fighting, and eating contests.

One of the most popular contests was log birling. This sport was invented by lumberjacks. Two men stood on opposite ends of the same floating log and rolled rapidly with their feet. Each birler tried to throw the other into the water. Each river had a champion birler.

An exciting birling contest took place in Ashland, Wisconsin. Who was the best birler in all the Lake States? Thousands of lumberjacks came to Ashland to find out.

A dozen men got through the first birling matches. Finally, only two were left: Tom Oliver, Michigan's best, and Jim Stewart, the pride of Wisconsin. The two men birled for nearly two days, with time out only for eating and sleeping. Each tried to trick the other with fancy footwork, twists, turns, and spins. Finally, Oliver toppled over from tiredness. Stewart received one hundred dollars prize money and a medal. He was the best man on logs.

Gay lumber towns became scenes of sadness when fire struck. Many towns were surrounded by forests. Left-over cuttings turned tinder-dry in hot weather. So did piles of sawdust and bits of lumber. Hot sparks from smokestacks, locomotives, or campfires could start a raging fire. The frame buildings and sidewalks burned like paper. Many sawmills kept barrels of water standing on their rooftops to put out fires.

One of the most famous of these fires was the Peshtigo fire in 1871. Peshtigo, Wisconsin was the headquarters of the Peshtigo Lumber Company. On an October day a strong wind sprang up. It fanned small fires that had been burning during the dry fall. FIRE! Church bells clanged out the dreaded warning. "It's coming fast!" people called. "It's a crown fire!" This meant that flames were racing along the tops of trees. Within an hour the whole town was wrapped in a tornado of fire.

Families dashed to throw themselves into the river. Oxen, horses, dogs, all followed their owners. Some people lowered themselves into wells. Others fell as the fire swept over them.

This old print shows the terrified townspeople of Peshtigo racing to the safety of the river.

Isaac Stephenson, a lumberman who became a United States Senator, was an owner of the lumber company. He described the result of the fire in the story of his life: "Every house was gone and only twisted ruins marked the places where the factory, mills, the supply store, and other buildings had been." The fire left a dozen communities in ashes, and over a thousand people dead.

Those who lived were left without shelter and without work. The burned-over land made poor farm land. Nevertheless, the people of Peshtigo worked hard and rebuilt their town. Cities far and near sent boatloads of food and clothing to help. In the late fall, the men of Peshtigo packed up their turkey sacks and left to find lumber camps and tall pines that fire had not touched.

So the seasons went, year after year. In autumn, the North Woods took on new life with the opening of lumber camps. In snow-time, the woods rang with the cutting and the cry of *timber-rrrrr*! In springtime, the rivers surged and foamed with the floating log drives. In summertime, lumber towns buzzed with the whine of sawmills and the laughter of spreeing lumberjacks.

There was hard work and danger. But there was fun too. Wherever there were lumberjacks, there was music and storytelling. Whereever there was storytelling by lumberjacks, there was the magical name of Paul Bunyan.

10. The Greatest Lumberjack of All

Paul Bunyan! You have heard of Paul.
He was the kingpin of them all—
The greatest logger in the land.

Round River Drive

Lumberjacks gave the world literature as well as lumber. Their imagination could run as wild as the wilderness they logged. Lumberjacks created the Paul Bunyan stories out of the way they lived. They gave Paul the abilities that they admired. He could do anything that called for strength or mastership.

Paul was big. He pulled up pine trees and used the branches to comb his beard. He crushed big boulders with his bare hands.

Paul was best man. He was the super logger, the boss foreman. He could outwork, outfight, outbirl, and outeat any lumberjack who ever lived.

Paul was gentle, though. He used his size and skill to improve logging, never to harm anyone. When he did fight, it was usually with an onery river, or perhaps with a crazy-crooked road or a stubborn mountain.

Night after night, lumberjacks sat on the deacon seat and matched tall tales about Ol' Paul. The caboose glowed. A cloud of steam rose from drying woolens. Smoke from pipes turned the bunkhouse a hazy blue. Every storyteller pretended that he had known and worked with Paul Bunyan. "Boys, did I ever tell you about the time Ol' Paul and I . . . ?" The storytelling session was on.

Paul did some of his best logging after the Winter of the Blue Snow. Did anyone ever tell you about that winter? Well, when the snowflakes flew down, they were not white, but blue. For forty days and forty nights it snowed. The whole countryside was covered with a snow-blanket, as blue as a robin's eggs. When the blue snow finally melted, smart folks got the bright idea of using the snow-water for ink. They began writing down stories about Ol' Paul, instead of telling them.

It was during the Winter of the Blue Snow that Paul found Babe. One day he saw a blue tail sticking out of a snowbank. Paul pulled. Out came a baby ox. The snow had turned it all blue. "Poor babe," Paul crooned. "I'll take you home for a pet." He named his pet Babe.

Babe stayed blue. He grew to be the biggest ox that ever skidded logs. Paul's pet crow, Jim, used to perch on Babe's left horn. One winter day Jim decided to fly across to the right horn. By the time he made it, the spring log drive was on.

Paul's biggest camp was on the Big Onion River. This was not far from the Little Garlic River. Paul used the nearby Big Fraid and Little Skeery Streams for log driving.

There were ten thousand lumberjacks in that Big Onion camp. It took a whole day to walk around the bunkhouse. Jacks floated up to their top bunks with balloons. They came down by parachutes. Paul always had four crews working. One crew was in the woods, one was going to work, one was coming home, and the fourth was eating.

Lumberjacks from just about every country came to work for Paul. Big Ole Olsen was the best blacksmith that ever burned iron. Hels Helsen was the woods foreman. Gun Gunderson, better known as Shot Gunderson, led the log drives. There were others: John Johnson, Criss Crosshaulsen, Murph Murpheson, Blue-Nose Parker, Batiste Joe, to name a few. Jonah Wiles was the camp grumbler and griper.

Food in Paul's camp was the best a lumberjack ever ate. Hot Biscuit Slim was the kingbee cook. He had good helpers too. Cream Puff Fatty made the desserts. Pea Soup Shorty stirred the stews and soups. Sourdough Sam baked the breads.

Sourdough Sam's flapjacks were so good that the jacks ate them faster than they could be flipped. Ole, the blacksmith, solved this problem. He made a flapjack griddle as wide as a good-sized lake. He invented a special mixer to make the batter. (If you want to know what it looked like, watch some cement workers. They copied Ole's model and now use it for mixing cement to build highways and skyscrapers.)

Cookees greased the griddle by skating around

88

and around the top with bacon strapped to their feet. Other cookees on horseback galloped around the tables, rolling flapjacks into plates with cant hooks. Sprinkler wagons followed to carry the syrup.

Paul's camp had the best clerk that ever worked in a wanigan. One day Paul and Babe strode across the Big Rock Candy Mountain. This was in the Smiling River Country, where the Big Sunny and the Little Smiley Rivers flowed. Paul came upon a man sitting on a hill, and putting figures on a piece of birch bark.

"What's your name?" Paul asked the stranger.

"Johnny Inkslinger," the stranger replied. "I am the man who invented figures."

Paul hired Johnny on the spot. Johnny Inkslinger kept records for thousands of lumberjacks and measurements for millions of logs. He never made a mistake. Johnny could hold three pencils in each hand and write down six rows of figures at the same time. When things got rushed, he added with one hand while he subtracted, divided, and multiplied with the other.

One year, Paul was logging pine where the Black Puppy and the White Puppy Streams flowed into the Yellow Dog River. An eagle carrier brought him a letter one day. It was from the King of Sweden. Paul sent for Ole, the Swede. "Tell me what the letter says," Paul ordered.

The letter said that the King of Sweden needed Paul's help. Thousands of Swedes needed land to grow wheat. Could Paul please log off a place for them in America?

Paul talked the matter over with his men. "It's against all reason!" Jonah the grumbler muttered as usual.

"It's possible!" the other men declared.

"Answer the King's letter," Paul ordered Ole. "Tell the Boss King of Sweden to send his people. We'll have the land logged."

Where could he put the people from Sweden? Paul thought and ate, and ate and thought. (The more Paul ate, the better he could think.) Suddenly the answer came to him. The Dakotas! North and South Dakota would be perfect for farming.

Paul and his mighty loggers set to work clearing the Dakotas to make room for farms. Paul invented the mile-long saw. Every time the cry of *"Timber-rrrrr!"* rang out, forty acres of pine fell. Babe skidded the logs as fast as the jacks could cut them.

The King sent Paul another letter. "Could Paul please drive the logs over the Atlantic to Sweden?" he asked. (He made Paul a side bet of fifty cents that it could not be done.)

Well! That was the longest log drive in history. Shot Gunderson led the river pigs through the Great Lakes, out the St. Lawrence River, and into the Atlantic Ocean. They made it in three weeks. They would have made it sooner, but they stopped when the King of England came out to visit. The English King had never seen an American log drive.

The Swedes came to the Dakotas. They had enough land to grow all the wheat they pleased. While the men had been away, Paul and Babe had straightened roads and sprinkled lakes here and there. The land looked real pretty. If you don't believe this, take a trip to the Dakotas. You won't find many pine trees. But you will find wheat farms.

Paul did not give up logging until the Spring of the Rain that Came up from China. Do you know about that spring? You've seen rain that falls down from the sky. Well, this year, rain hissed UP from the ground. But that's another long story. There are stories and stories about Ol' Paul and his mighty lumberjacks. Read them all. Other storytellers added on to the tales that the lumberjacks started.

You can learn a lot about people from their stories. Paul Bunyan is a symbol of the strength and bigness that is America. When you understand the spirit of the Paul Bunyan stories, you will understand the American lumberjack. You will also begin to understand America—the real America.

The heydey of lumbering in the Lake States ended by 1900. Lumbermen began cutting the pine in the Pacific Northwest. The lumberjacks once again followed the pines. Their colorful and courageous reign as kings in the North

Woods was over. They had ruled well, with ax and saw, cant hook and peavey. These heroes of young America let "daylight in the swamps." They opened up the country to make room for the future.

Their story will not be forgotten. Lumberjacks will be remembered as long as shanty ballads are sung and Paul Bunyan tales are told. This should be as long as forever.

Glossary

bateau: a light, swift boat

boom: a floating corral for holding logs

breech loader: a bunk which was entered from the side

bucker: the lumberjack who cut trees into log lengths

bull cook: the camp handyman

bull of the woods: foreman of the camp

cant hook: a tool used for loading logs

cookee: cook's helper

deacon seat: a bench in the bunkhouse used in place of chairs

faller: the lumberjack who felled trees

Gabriel: a long tin horn used to summon lumberjacks

go-devil: a sled for moving logs out of the forest

greenhorn: an inexperienced lumberjack or a recent immigrant

inkslinger: a logging camp clerk and timekeeper

iron burner: a blacksmith

log birling: log rolling, a sport invented by lumberjacks

log drive: the floating of logs downriver in spring

log jam: the piling up of logs on the drive

log mark: a brand stamped on logs to show ownership

log skidding: log hauling

muzzle loader: a bunk entered from the end

nosebag: a lumberjack's lunch bag used while on a log drive

peavey: a tool used to handle logs on the drive

pike pole: a tool used to direct floating logs

river pig: a lumberjack who drove logs downriver

road monkey: a lumberjack who kept logging roads in good shape

shanty: the bunkhouse in which lumberjacks slept

shanty-boy: a lumberjack

skidder: a lumberjack who hauled logs from the forest

sky-loader: the man who stood on top of the pile of logs while a sleigh was loaded

sky pilot: a preacher who visited lumber camps

sourdough stiff: a camp cook

sprinkler: a device used to haul water and make ice roads

swamper: the lumberjack who cut the limbs off logs and kept the forest floor cleared

teamster: the lumberjack who drove the logging sleigh and the supply wagon

timber cruiser: a woodsman who explored forests for good trees

tote road: a road over which supplies were hauled

wanigan: the camp supply store and office; on the drive, the cook shanty

wood butcher: a carpenter

Index

A
Animals
  forest, 43, 44
  horses, 30, 31 (pic), 32 (pic), 34
  imaginary, 54, 55
  oxen, 30 (pic), 31, 32, 34

B
Bateaux, 70
Bohn, Dr. Frank, 61, 62
Bunkhouse, 15
  bunks, 15, 16, 27 (pic)
  caboose, 21
  deacon seat, 16, 21, 27 (pic)
Bunyan, Paul, 7, 8, 85–92

C
Carlson, Pete, 46
Clothing, 21, 22, 27, 66, 79
Cook shanty, 16 (pic), 38, 41–43, 41 (pic), 42 (pic)

D
Doctors, 61, 62

E
Entertainment, 80
  contests, 81
  dancing, 49–50
  fighting, 80
  games, 50–52
  singing, 46, 48–50, 52–54
  storytelling, 54

F
Fires, 82, 83
Fredrickson, Nels, 45

G
Gabriel, 20 (pic), 22, 25, 41
Go-devil, 31 (pic)
Greenhorns, 50, 51, 54

H
Higgins, Rev. Frank, 62, 63
"Hurrah," 49, 51, 52, 54, 55

I
Immigrants, 18, 19, 50
Indians, 13, 43, 70

J
Johnson, Ole, 46

L
Lake States, 9, 11, 18, 19, 29, 92
Language, 14, 29
Laundry, 56, 57 (pic)
Log birling, 81
  Oliver, Tom, 81
  Stewart, Jim, 81
Log drive, 65–76

Logging road, 17, 30
Log jams, 72, 73 (pic), 74–76
Log marks, 34 (pic), 76
Logs, 25 (pic), 29, 30, 31 (pic), 32 (pic), 35, 65, 66
Log skidding, 32, 35
Lumber camp, 14, 15 (pic), 16, 18, 45
  blacksmith shop, 16
  bunkhouse, 15, 16, 21, 27 (pic)
  cook shanty, 16 (pic), 38, 41–43, 41 (pic), 42 (pic)
  office, 16
  stable, 16
  supply store, 16
Lumber company, 13, 14, 34
Lumberjacks
  blacksmiths, 14, 17 (pic)
  buckers, 25
  cant hook men, 32
  carpenters, 14, 16, 17
  clerk, 58
  cook, 37–39, 41 (pic), 43, 66
  cookees, 38, 39, 41 (pic), 42, 71
  fallers, 24
  foremen, 14, 22, 35, 37, 38, 61
  river pigs, 65, 66, 67 (pic), 68, 70–76

road monkeys, 33, 34
skidders, 30 (pic), 31 (pic)
sky-loader, 32 (pic), 33
swampers, 25
teamsters, 17, 32, 33
timber cruisers, 12 (pic), 13, 14
Lumber towns, 77, 82

M

Magazines and newspapers, 60
Maybee, Rolland, 48
Meals, 22, 25, 26 (pic), 39–44, 42 (pic), 71
Michigan, 8, 11, 30
Minnesota, 8, 11, 30

N

North Woods, 7, 8, 11, 84, 92
Nose bags, 71

P

Peavey, Joseph, 67
Peshtigo Lumber Company, 82
Peshtigo, Wisconsin, 9, 82, 83 (pic), 84
Pineries, 11
Pioneers, 10 (pic)
Preachers, 62–64

R

Red Sash Brigade, 79
River pigs, 65, 66, 67 (pic), 68, 70–76
Road monkeys, 33, 34

S

Saginaw, Michigan, 9, 77, 78
Sands, Louie, 45, 46
Sawmills, 9, 29, 78, 82
Skidways, 32
Songs and rhymes, 7, 20, 29, 36, 37, 41, 46, 53, 75, 76, 85

Sorting boom, 76
Stephenson, Isaac, 83
Superstitions, 14, 72
Supplies, 17, 58

T

Tools, 17, 18 (pic), 24
cant hooks, 17 (pic), 32 (pic)
crosscut saws, 17 (pic), 24, 25 (pic)
peaveys, 67, 68, 70, 74
pike poles, 67
Tote roads, 16, 17
Trees
cedar, 16
poplar, 14
white pine, 10, 11, 13, 22
Turkey sacks, 19

W

Wanigan, 58, 66, 71 (pic), 72
Wisconsin, 8, 11, 30

96

DATE DUE			
DEC 8	21		
SEP 9	25		
DEC 12	22		
OCT 5	10		
T	28		
NOV 15	27		
MAR 14	41		

HIGHSMITH 45-220